I Wore the Only Garden I've Ever Grown

I Wore the Only Garden I've Ever Grown

Kathryn Leland

HEADMISTRESS PRESS

Copyright © 2017 by Kathryn Leland
All rights reserved.

ISBN-13: 978-0997914955
ISBN-10: 0997914955

This book may not be reproduced, in whole or in part, including illustrations, in any form (beyond that permitted by Sections 107 and 108 of the U.S. Copyright Law and except by reviewers for the public press), without written permission from the publishers.

Cover art by Lisa Congdon http://www.lisacongdon.com
Book design by Mary Meriam

PUBLISHER
Headmistress Press
60 Shipview Lane
Sequim, WA 98382
Telephone: 917-428-8312
Email: headmistresspress@gmail.com
Website: headmistresspress.blogspot.com

for Corinne Julia & Brady Nate

Contents

At 22, Night Terrors Again	1
I Wore the Only Garden I've Ever Grown	2
My Favorite Dad Story	3
Sticks & Stones May	4
When I Say My Mother Can't Cook	5
No Evidence of Cancer	6
The Worst Thing I Never Did for My Little Sister	7
To My Baby Brother on the Day You Are Finally Taller Than Me	8
Shedding Memory	9
Forty Years an Ex-Ballerina	10
Lights & Cameras – A Short Film	11
The Month We Tried to Die & Why We've Never Talked About It	14
Affinity	15
The Same Images	16
A Little Girl's Plea	17
A Prayer for My Father	19
Shedding Names	20
Phone Call at Kitchen Sinks	21
About the Author	23

At 22, Night Terrors Again

I woke alone in my apartment cellophane-wrapped
in hot, stuck sheets. I'd wet the bed.
Dead and dumb with sleep at 3 AM, I stumbled
down the hall to wash quilts and ammoniaed
bedclothes. In the community laundry room, I fell
asleep against the washing machine, dreamt in and out of a night
fifteen years ago when I woke in the bathtub
covered in my sister's piss. Our skin adhered together
by the cold, soaked flannel of her pajamas. Our mother
asleep, her body barricading the bathroom door, cordless
phone receiver cradled on her pregnant belly. Our father was
somewhere in the glass-still house. I tried to stay so still, her urine
itching my skin like so many ants as I waited
for the bathroom door to bow inward again, distend
into the room from my father's weight
on the other side. Silence this fragile could do nothing
but break.

I Wore the Only Garden I've Ever Grown

The first time, he called it an accident: when I failed
twice to appear after he'd hollered up the stairs
for me and his hands left

purple thumbs of Aster and palm-beds of burgundy
Dahlia, blooming bright around my arm
for weeks until a broken dish, a new

reason to coax blooms from the bluish leaves layered
like petals down my arms. Alone, I watched the flowers
age to a soft, custard yellow that faded in to my skin

under blue jeans and long sleeves. The flowers bloomed,
dried, and crushed to dust. All the evidence hushed and
blown away like dandelion feathers.

My Favorite Dad Story

Barbie, I hope you die of a fucking heart attack like your dad.

Why don't you just go back up into the mountains and drink yourself to sleep, Mark?

[from an argument between my parents, heard through the bedroom door circa 2000]

At nineteen, he dropped out of college. Decided he needed to be in Alaska with cold streams of King Salmon to pillage and green spruce trees tall enough to make his six-foot-three frame feel like something even bigger. He only made it as far as Denver where he ran out of money and spent a year living in a tent behind a Mexican-food restaurant washing dishes for his dinner.

The day he taught me to ski, he told me that in Denver, he filled donuts with custard and jam pouring out of a long pipe neck from the ceiling of a pastry shop, said he made just enough money to ski every day there was snow.

There's only one photo from that whole year he was in Colorado. He's on a mountain, surrounded by all that white, laughing from the left corner of the frame with his mouth open wide. Navy and green ski coat, and knit cap over long curls.

He is bald now, but under all that hair he used to have, I don't think he knew he would make it back to school, to New York City and a real reporting job, out on a blind date, grilled cheese and tomato soup with my mother. I have to believe he didn't know what he would do to us.

Sticks & Stones May

On stale Sunday afternoons, shut tight inside your house until 5 PM (but usually later), I could know what kind of day it was going to be by your first cup of coffee, by how hard things hit the countertops, and if you were laughing to yourself at jokes I didn't understand. When your back was turned, I would tip my nose over the edge of your mug.

On those whiskey-slipped days, you pretended to write while you lost village after village on Age of Empires to fire and famine. Sleeping on the sofa, long past the hour you were told to have us home, those days were better. Better to whisper around that house all day because you were sleeping than because it could be any of the next words or thumping stair steps that set you off.

Trapped upstairs in that cold-smelling house, it tasted like lamplight with the blinds perpetually closed, and I even tried to breathe quietly. I wasn't ever quiet enough to keep you from finding some reason to sway up the stairs after me. And I remember thinking, on those days, with your face a centimeter from mine, your hands pressing me hard against a wall,

I wish you would just go ahead and break my arm.

This poem, etched instead as the spiral crack of radius or ulna, the proof would be so loud I would never have to say what you had done.

When I Say My Mother Can't Cook

what I mean is that she is an Olympic gold-medalist
in toast burning, a seasoned connoisseur
of crunchy cookies, and someone who believes
in the racial equality of pancakes. I say this, but
I cannot remember a single Thanksgiving after
she left our father when her table wasn't so
full that we ran out of chairs. My brother, sister,
and I sat on the coffee table like it was a bench
and ate turkey and green beans from plates
on our lap next to authors and young publicists with
their semi-pro golfer boyfriends, a woman who
called herself our Italian aunt and her
cancer-researching husband who used to make
Irish Potatoes: mashed without butter or salt.
I remember my mother getting up over and
over again to refill the butter dish while I
watched every person at that table melt
pats of butter over mounds of wet starch. And I say
my mother can't cook, but what I mean is that
this matters much less than her wide table.

No Evidence of Cancer

At a beach town grocery store, between aisles
of cat food and corn chips, you told us
easy as dropping a package of paper napkins in

the cart, that you'd once had
cancer. No lead-up or drama, just
in passing, because it was gone

now. Driving us home, I dissect the truth: how
you'd slunk off on the weekends we were
with our father and hid your treatment

the way other women hide affairs. How you drove
yourself to the hospital to cut away the part of you
that slid me, pink and soft, into this world.

The last evidence I once fit snug
in your belly. Because now, I am so tall
that you try to hold me and your bird-bone frame can only

fit ducked beneath my chin. It does not matter
that I was the first person you'd ever met to share
your genes. You were adopted because your mother cut

you out of her story and now you have cut me out
of yours. So when you told us
about your cancer, my sister cried

and I walked away.

The Worst Thing I Never Did for My Little Sister

The Halloween they brought you home from the
hospital – a long, yellow wax bean in a knit pumpkin cap –
I lined up all my baby dolls against the wall of our shared

bedroom with their small plush feet pressed against the wall
and told Mom they were in time-out because *babies are bad.*
They thought I was going to smother you in your crib.

Sometimes, I think you might have been better off if I had.

To My Baby Brother on the Day You Are Finally Taller Than Me

Even though I was four and a half feet tall before you were one cell
high, everyone told me that one day you would be able

to look down at me like I was something small. Everyone was
almost certainly right. But on that day, I will still remember

the night in the backseat of our mother's
parked car when I thumbed the rind

off my eight-year-old heart and gave it
to you, not section by section, but all

at once. Dropped it on the grey carpet, soft
as the backside of Velcro, to roll in cracker dust

with lost sippy cups of chunky milk, around and
over our sister's bare feet. The translucent

skinned sections still adhered together, whole and
perfect. And Brady, I pressed you to my chest like I could

hold you inside my empty ribcage, safe
from the sirens screaming through

the back window and our father
denting the hood of the car with

fists like falling unripe fruit, safe from
a night you can't even remember.

Shedding Memory

Last Christmas, my mother ran her thumb and index over one
of my curls, pulling it gently so it sprang back against the tendons in
my neck, asking, *When was the last time you cut this mess?* I threaded
my fingers into my bundle of spirals, always lighter in color, never perfect
and straight like hers.

I know it's been too long but I imagine silver scissors slipping across
that ragged hem, and remember what I lose. My skin is
sloughing off cells hourly, but I wore those strands winning
swimming medals, letting my first girlfriend run fingertips through. Like rings
on a tree, the oldest bands have been soaked in Canadian lakes and trapped
smoke in Irish bars.

The month I first wrote about my father, I started snipping. Left
fine brown crosshatching on the surface of my desk. Just a
little, almost everyday. I let the memories sit
there, in a pile. Absently running fingertips over the tiny
heaps. Glad to have them off my head as I sift for the
reason he wound his hands into these little strings and swung
my marionette skull into the side of the bannister.

I need to know the answer
was in his hands, not my hair; in who
he is, not who I am.

Forty Years an Ex-Ballerina

> *Once you lose someone it is never exactly*
> *the same person who comes back.*
> — Sharon Olds

The day I taught my mother how to hop a chain link fence
she wore ballet slippers—the only pair she didn't burn after she'd ripped
the ribbon of tendon running up her leg. It was the second time I saw her

dance, but the only time she'd worn them since they told her she wasn't
going to be a dancer anymore. Watching her that day, I thought it would be
like time traveling. I thought I would be able to see the woman she was

before she got hurt. I realize I'd always thought of her as two women, the one
she was before and the person she became after. But now the woman I see
dancing is the same one I have always known and I wonder if she is the same
continuous woman or if something

happened to never let her be that person again. The first time
she danced for me was a Thursday while my brother played piano. She
slipped across the carpet like a flame I don't remember being lit.
    And I wish I'd

asked her then, *don't you feel like smoke?* I think of it rising off the burning
slippers and skirts, the photographs (I never saw)
of a woman I can't tell if I've ever met.

Lights & Cameras – A Short Film

Scene: *Adult sisters, Kate & Corey, tape a black sheet to a wall of their parents' home. The sheet is the one Kate slept on in high school. There is a baby grand piano that takes up most of the room. Canvases from Ikea hang on the pale blue walls. Studio lights rest on the piano bench, a bookshelf, and another is duct-taped to a tripod. Kate is in a kitchen chair with a Canon AE-1 35mm and Corey is on a stool that belongs upstairs. Before they start, Corey says this reminds her of the staged dance recital photos they used to have taken—posed on a little painted stepstool in a stiff tulle skirt: red or yellow or mint green. Tonight, their parents are already gone to bed. Their kid brother is out with his friends. They are probably in a Sonic parking lot drinking watermelon slushes. While she photographs, Kate asks Corey questions.*

I don't like these questions, Kate. It's a weird
conversation to have with your sister. Like hmmm... let me
think of my childhood that you were there for... I guess
the story I always tell is the one about the time we
rolled a watermelon down the stairs and it
exploded all over the carpet – which, it's just
amazing that it happened and maybe that's why I
like it. That, and it's a moment. Because, I mean, those are
what make a good story.

> *[I don't even really remember the watermelon. Just the years
> afterward, burying our noses in the carpet at the foot of the stairs
> and swearing that it still smelled like sweet, wet fruit, the Fourth of July,
> and sawdust.]*

The first thing I wanted to be when I grew up? Oh, I don't
remember. I definitely had a weird idea that, even though I never – well
I guess I believed in a God for a very short period of time, but I
was just very certain that my life, like everyone else I knew
in suburbia, was designed in a very specific way. I would fall
in love at the appropriate age and I would get a job
at the appropriate age and I would go to a good college
because I wasn't stupid but I didn't really have a dream or a plan.

> *[In high school, I used to drive you home
> from school the long way, a loop of highway that
> skirted the city limits. I would turn at the last
> second every day pretending that this time we wouldn't
> go home. All I ever wanted was to run
> away. I want to ask if you felt the
> same way back then, but I don't.]*

They stop to move the lights around. Corey talks about the last set she was on; how she was both the stand-in for a child actor and asked to hold a pole up for twenty minutes so it didn't fall into the scene. She says it's kind of like this, light crew and subject. They argue about film v. digital. It's a generational argument they're too young to have but it makes them feel like artists.

I never stuck with any hobbies ever. I played
piano, I liked architecture, and I read books but not
enough to think I qualify for the "nerdy kid who grew
up reading books" club which is a metaphorical thing that
exists, and I joined every club that you joined. So I
was in orchestra and I was on swim team and…
then I joined my school's broadcast team with some friends.

> *[I remember you following me around, like the shadow I was never
> going to live up to. Always stretched into godly proportion behind
> me. You don't tell me about the moment you fell
> in love with film, like that's too private. I wish I had better
> answers for you about why we swam.]*

My whole current concern is like not knowing
what I want. I feel like that's a very like college thing.
Cause I'm not sure I like my major… as much as I should.
Do you every think you like something because you think
you're supposed to like it or you like the idea of liking it?
Or even like, its stupid things; if I forget anything
that's relevant to film I'm like okay well you really remember
the things you care about, right? Like even if you barely heard
it, like it was just mentioned to you in passing, if it's something
you really care about you're gonna remember it.

> *[You have to remember those years before mom and dad were divorced. Brady was too young, but I know you remember.]*

So when I forget things
about film, like I forget all the
time, settings on my camera and
stuff, I'm worried that it's
a reflection I don't really
care about it. That it doesn't matter and
it wasn't real.

> *[What I need to know is that he didn't ever hit you after I left. When I asked you, two years ago, you said he never did. But say it again. Say that you wrote me poems about how he swallowed you like a whale but it doesn't mean what I think it does.]*

Can we be
done now?

The Month We Tried to Die
& Why We've Never Talked About It

Brady, the night you told Mom you couldn't be
a person anymore, I wasn't down the hall, reading
on my blue beanbag chair; we didn't have
breakfast together just that morning, cold
Pop-Tarts in the silence of a dark car; and I didn't
pick you up from soccer practice that day either. Because I
was eight hours away at college, on my
girlfriend's twin-sized dorm bed, making up stories
to cover the skin I'd burned off the backs
of my hands. You were fourteen that month, and I was
twenty, and I could drive home for you but the six and a half
years between us is getting bigger every hour
I am away. Brady, I don't know how to tell you
that you are not alone because even when you are close enough
to touch, it is like my fingertips can barely even brush
the skin of your shoulder blades.

Affin·i·ty

> *n. a spontaneous or natural liking or sympathy for someone or something. relationship, especially by marriage as opposed to blood ties.*

My brother says he's going through a phase
where he doesn't think he looks like any of
us. He told Mom, *But maybe it's that I look just like
your dad.* And what if he does? There could be

a 70-year-old man in Indiana wearing my brother's
face as he drinks gas station coffee behind
the wheel of a box truck. This is wild to me, but
not so much so as the last time I was home,

when we ate breakfast together before I dropped
him off at school. He reminded me so much of
the man who raised our mother, the grandfather who
used to eat breakfast with me while everyone else slept

in. Silently sharing a split grapefruit, I realize that
under the citrus sprays of red fruit is that same Old Spice scent.
That combination and way he lifts the dripping sections to
his mouth on the end of a butter knife is almost uncanny.

The Same Images

My sister and I both write poems where we make our bodies
wooden and our hearts into fruit. Like we need to be made
of something more certain of its age and more clear in its toughness

than skin is; like we think our heart is something to be eaten
out of our chest. Corey, do you remember how we used to swim
together in the bathtub? Do you remember playing

Barbie in bubble baths, your favorite one with pink and
blonde hair, and the stories you used to write about her
like she was someone you knew

> *at night she dreams of strawberry farms and*
> *the families that live on them. She watches*
> *the children running through their fields,*
> *getting juice stains down the front of their*
> *shirts, laughing with the grasshoppers and*
> *collecting fireflies at night.*

Corey, for years, we watched our mother build her body out of nothing
but iceberg lettuce and black tea. I want to cram our too long bodies back
into that bathtub and tell you, with hot water up to our ribcages, that you are

made of freckled skin and hard bone, of a father who hit us and a mother
who was afraid. I want to tell you that I can't stop your skin from tearing but
I know how to sew. I can't promise you'll learn anything from writing

but if you make a body for yourself out of paper, they can burn it, tear it,
throw it away, but you will always be able to write yourself a new one.

A Little Girl's Plea

I.

She was holding my brother tight
inside her body, while my father held hard
the thin, jawed edge of her face and
flecked her cheeks with freckle-spots
of saliva and whiskey. Upstairs I slept

through the thump of her head
against a wall and the groan
of the fence – my father
swinging his body over,
fleeing to the neighbor's yard.

II.

She tells me this story three days before Independence Day the year I am twenty-one. At a New York City hotel's rooftop bar over our fourth or fifth glasses of wine, she finally says how he split her lip and left her concussed body on the kitchen floor that night, sixteen years ago now. Then, under a sky so choked with light that the stars are smeared to hazy yellow, she tells me she knew, has always known, that my father hit me. She admits she saw the bruises on my body. And I know what she is saying is that she also saw my long arms, thought maybe I could wrap myself around my brother and sister, that I could protect them like she couldn't. And I want to hate her

III.

for every indigo thumbprint, for every
staircase I was thrown down, for every finger on my
right hand the afternoon my father decided a reasonable
punishment for losing my sweater on the playground
was to stand in the doorway of his bedroom gripping
the doorframe while he slammed twelve times, once
for every dollar the sweater cost. I want to hate her

IV.

except that you cannot imagine how small she looks when she says it. Small like thin but also like young. Like, I can see the seams inside of her that are splitting even while they are supposed to be holding her together. Splitting enough to let a sixteen-year-old secret worm its way out. Years have worn her thin, but right now it's like I can see the little girl she used to be. I want to hate her but instead I hold her. Because she was wrong.

V.

When I was sixteen, I called my father from a swim meet in Round Rock, TX and told him through asthmatic breaths that I did not care, ever since bruises became hard to hide under a swimsuit, how careful he had been to hit with open hands, today I was done. Over his cool laughter and promises that no one would believe anything I said about him, I told him that I wouldn't see him ever again. What I meant was

I am selfish. I would let my brother and my sister spend weekends in his house and pretend I did not know that he would pick one of them to start hitting instead.

VI.

So I hold my mother on a rooftop in the city where she met my father, where this all began, and realize I do not get to hate her. We have created a legacy of women leaving and lying and letting this happen and I don't know what is worst.

A Prayer for My Father

For you, my father who wrote us bedtime stories in green ink on a
yellow legal pad about a boy named Mark with a magic

toolbox; who played the same song on silk and steel strings so
many times for me that it sounded wrong when I finally heard

Rocky Raccoon on the radio – I thought you'd written that too. For
my father who used to take us driving through the Technicolor

Hill Country in spring. Bluebonnets and Indian Paintbrushes,
Mexican Hats and Wine Cups poking up through wooden-slatted stairs

down to clear-bottom swimming holes where we used to dive
for handfuls of clay and bottle caps rusted orange.

For my father feeding dark red worms onto silver hooks; for teaching us
to lurk in the back of a bookstore for hours. For the man, sitting

at his computer all night, trying to write,
I am trying too but I am not trying to hurt you.

All I want is to say into the silence,
This happened, all of it.

Shedding Names

Every second, my cells are cycling
away. Meaning I am always becoming
less and less the little girl
that I was. The one who said,

No, my daddy never hit me,

has started saying, *This happened.* Told my father, *I
remember.* And this year, right now,
this is the year that my mother finally took
my stepfather's name. The year my sister signed
a piece of paper saying my grandfather's
is the family name she'll keep.
This year, this is the year I'll do
the same. And while we carve apart
our names, shedding the pieces
of ourselves that still bear his shine, I say
this is year we stop letting him be
the most important thing that ever happened to us.

Phone Call at Kitchen Sinks

Last night, I told my mother I was trying
to marinate chicken breasts in Italian dressing and
edit a paper on *Satan Says*. I was completely unsure which
I was less qualified to do. I didn't know how to make
this dead muscle, split from a broken body, into
dinner, or how to cut apart then sew back together this
paper into anything but a confessional. She told me, over the sound
of water running in Texas, that I was *indomitable*. And burning
my knuckles on hot water and dish soap, phone cradled
between jaw bone and shirt collar, maybe we aren't
at the place where I tell her about my coffee date last week or
how drunk I got on a Wednesday night. But we are somehow
becoming two women holding each other up
like the telephone wire running five hundred miles
between Arkansas and Austin. I don't know how
to say this. So I tell her that there is rosemary growing
in a teacup next to my kitchen sink; how I pulled it off a bush
in front of my apartment building and that I've been watching it,
for weeks, build thin white roots into clear water.

About the Author

Kathryn Leland grew up in Austin, Texas. She received her BA in English – Creative Writing from Hendrix College and now works as an Editorial Assistant with Sibling Rivalry Press. She currently lives in central Arkansas.

Headmistress Press Books

Lovely - Lesléa Newman
Teeth & Teeth - Robin Reagler
How Distant the City - Freesia McKee
Shopgirls - Marissa Higgins
Riddle - Diane Fortney
When She Woke She Was an Open Field - Hilary Brown
God With Us - Amy Lauren
A Crown of Violets - Renée Vivien tr. Samantha Pious
Fireworks in the Graveyard - Joy Ladin
Social Dance - Carolyn Boll
The Force of Gratitude - Janice Gould
Spine - Sarah Caulfield
I Wore the Only Garden I've Ever Grown - Kathryn Leland
Diatribe from the Library - Farrell Greenwald Brenner
Blind Girl Grunt - Constance Merritt
Acid and Tender - Jen Rouse
Beautiful Machinery - Wendy DeGroat
Odd Mercy - Gail Thomas
The Great Scissor Hunt - Jessica K. Hylton
A Bracelet of Honeybees - Lynn Strongin
Whirlwind @ Lesbos - Risa Denenberg
The Body's Alphabet - Ann Tweedy
First name Barbie last name Doll - Maureen Bocka
Heaven to Me - Abe Louise Young
Sticky - Carter Steinmann
Tiger Laughs When You Push - Ruth Lehrer
Night Ringing - Laura Foley
Paper Cranes - Dinah Dietrich
On Loving a Saudi Girl - Carina Yun
The Burn Poems - Lynn Strongin
I Carry My Mother - Lesléa Newman
Distant Music - Joan Annsfire
The Awful Suicidal Swans - Flower Conroy
Joy Street - Laura Foley
Chiaroscuro Kisses - G.L. Morrison
The Lillian Trilogy - Mary Meriam
Lady of the Moon - Amy Lowell, Lillian Faderman, Mary Meriam
Irresistible Sonnets - ed. Mary Meriam
Lavender Review - ed. Mary Meriam

www.ingramcontent.com/pod-product-compliance
Lightning Source LLC
Chambersburg PA
CBHW070049070426
42449CB00012BA/3202